BAKER & TAYLOR

JESSE JAMES

REVISED EDITION

WANTED
DEAD OR ALIVE

By Carl R. Green and William R. Sanford

Enslow Publishers, Inc.
40 Industrial Road
Box 398
Berkeley Heights, NJ 07922
USA

http://www.enslow.com

Original edition published in 1992.

Library of Congress Cataloging-in-Publication Data
Green, Carl R.
 Jesse James / Carl R. Green and William R. Sanford. — Rev. ed.
    p. cm. — (Outlaws and lawmen of the wild West)
 Summary: "A look at the life of the outlaw Jesse James. Provides
further reading and Internet addresses"—Provided by publisher.
 Includes bibliographical references and index.
 ISBN 978-0-7660-3172-2
 1. James, Jesse, 1847–1882—Juvenile literature. 2. Outlaws—West
(U.S.)—Biography—Juvenile literature. 3. Frontier and pioneer
life—West (U.S.)—Juvenile literature. 4. West (U.S.)—History—
1860–1890—Juvenile literature. 5. West (U.S.)—Biography—Juvenile
literature. I. Sanford, William R. (William
Reynolds), 1927– II. Title.
 F594.J27G74 2009
 364.15'52092—dc22
 [B]
                          2008010008

 ISBN-10: 0-7660-3172-1

Printed in the United States of America

10 9 8 7 6 5 4 3 2 1

To Our Readers:
We have done our best to make sure all Internet Addresses in this book were active and appropriate when we went to press. However, the authors and the publisher have no control over and assume no liability for the material available on those Internet sites or on other Web sites they may link to. Any comments or suggestions can be sent by e-mail to comments@enslow.com or to the address on the back cover.

♻ Enslow Publishers, Inc., is committed to printing our books on recycled paper. The paper in every book contains 10% to 30% post-consumer waste (PCW). The cover board on the outside of each book contains 100% PCW. Our goal is to do our part to help young people and the environment too!

Interior photos: Alamy/Mary Evans Picture Library, p. 36; Alamy/Lordprice Collection, p. 38; Associated Press, p. 19; Bridgeman Art Library/Private Collection, Peter Newark American Pictures, pp. 26, 44; Cardcow.com, p. 16; Courtesy of Edward M. Bogard, p.17; The Granger Collection, New York, pp. 5, 7, 10, 20, 23, 29, 33; iStockphoto/spxChrome (marshal badge), odd pages; iStockphoto/Alex Bramwell (revolver), even pages; iStockphoto/billnoll (frame), pp. 4, 8, 11, 36; Legends of America, pp. 1, 11, 13, 25, 27, 34, 42; Library of Congress, p. 41; Minnesota Historical Society, pp. 30; North Wind/North Wind Archives, p. 24; Shutterstock/Dhoxax (background), pp. 3, 5, 8–9, 15, 22–23, 29, 36–37, 43; State Historical Society of Missouri, p. 8.

Cover photo: Legends of America (*Jesse James had this portrait taken in Missouri in 1864, when he was seventeen years old. He was already a veteran of the Civil War.*)

TABLE OF CONTENTS

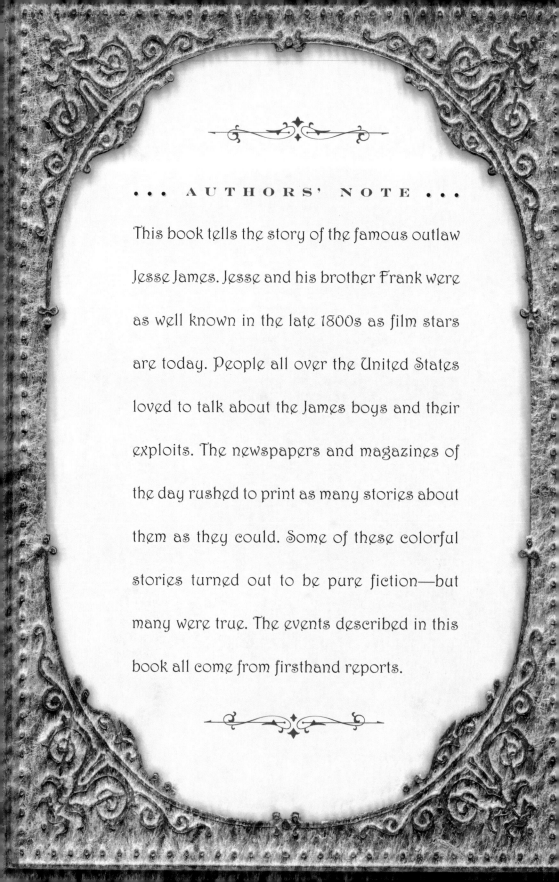

... AUTHORS' NOTE ...

This book tells the story of the famous outlaw Jesse James. Jesse and his brother Frank were as well known in the late 1800s as film stars are today. People all over the United States loved to talk about the James boys and their exploits. The newspapers and magazines of the day rushed to print as many stories about them as they could. Some of these colorful stories turned out to be pure fiction—but many were true. The events described in this book all come from firsthand reports.

JESSE AND THE WIDOW

Jesse James was a well-known outlaw and a gunslinger. Although he made his living by robbing banks and trains, Jesse did not think of himself as an evil man. It did not upset him to shoot someone during a robbery. "The fool should not have tried to stop us," Jesse would tell his friends.

During the 1800s, big business was hated and feared. So what if Jesse robbed banks and trains? That did

Even though he was a criminal, Jesse James was thought of as a hero by many. He is pictured here as a teenager.

not worry poor people. A great many of them admired Jesse and his gang.

The belief that Jesse James was a hero grew out of stories that cannot be proven. Even so, many Americans believed them. One popular tale tells about Jesse and a young widow.

Once, the story goes, Jesse's gang stopped at a farmhouse and asked for food. The widow who lived there fixed them a fine meal. As he ate, Jesse saw the woman crying. She told him that her husband had been killed in the Civil War. Left alone with young children to raise, she could not pay her debts. A heartless banker was coming to take away her farm later that day.

Jesse gave the woman the money she needed. Be sure, he told her, to get a signed receipt from the banker. That will be proof that you paid him, he explained. Then he and the boys rode off.

When the banker arrived, the widow handed him the money. That enraged the man, for he had planned to take over her farm. Angrily, he took the money and wrote out a receipt. Later, when he left the farm, Jesse and his gang waylaid him. After he calmly emptied the man's pockets, Jesse waved and rode away.

In the 1800s, many people distrusted big business, including railroads. That often made heroes out of the outlaws who robbed them, such as Jesse James. This 1879 cartoon pokes fun at Cornelius Vanderbilt and his fellow railroad owners.

Is the story true? Most experts doubt that it happened. The record shows that Jesse James was no Robin Hood. He did not take from the rich and give to the poor. What he stole, he kept for himself.

CHAPTER TWO

GROWING UP IN HARD TIMES

Much of western Missouri was still raw frontier in the mid-1800s. Life was hard. People were more likely to die of disease or gunshot wounds than of old age. If Jesse James grew up to be an outlaw, the times helped make him so.

Jesse's father, Robert James, was a preacher. Robert married Zerelda Cole in 1842. The young couple then moved to a farm near Kearney

Jesse's father, Robert, was a preacher. He died just before Jesse's third birthday.

in western Missouri. Reverend James preached in the New Hope Baptist Church on Sundays. During the week, he and Zerelda ran the farm with the help of black slaves.

Frank, the James's first child, was born in 1843. A second son died soon after birth. Jesse Woodson James was born in 1847. His sister Susan arrived two years later.

Reverend James was well-liked around Kearney. He even found time to help start a college in the area. The call of the newly-opened gold fields was too much for him, however. Robert James headed west in 1850 to "strike it rich." Three weeks later he fell ill and died.

Zerelda James soon wed Ben Simms. When Frank and Jesse refused to obey their stepfather, Simms moved out. In 1855, Zerelda married Dr. Reuben Samuel. Dr. Samuel was a gentle man. He let the James boys do pretty much what they wished.

Over the next few years, Zerelda gave birth to four more babies. The seven children all lived on the Samuel farm. In normal times, the boys might have grown up to become farmers, too.

In the 1850s, the times were far from normal. The people of Missouri were mostly Southerners who wanted to keep slaves. Many of them believed Kansas

Quantrill's Raiders were guerrillas from Missouri who burned towns and farms in Kansas. This conflict over slavery merged with the Civil War when the fighting started.

should be a slave state, too. Fighting broke out when antislave farmers moved into Kansas. Armed bands from Missouri raided the new settlements. Houses were burned and people were gunned down on both sides.

In 1861, the fighting in Kansas merged with the outbreak of the Civil War. The "war between the states" started when the southern states tried to leave the United States. The North went to war to save the Union. Missouri was torn between staying in the Union and joining the South. In the end, the state stayed loyal. Zerelda Samuel's heart, however, belonged to the South. She was pleased when Frank left to join the rebel army.

Young Frank soon came down with measles. Captured by Union troops, he promised to stay out of the fighting. That pledge earned him a safe trip home. Soon, however, a Union general ordered all young men to join the state militia.

William Quantrill was the leader of Quantrill's Raiders. He died in battle in 1865.

Frank refused. Rather than fight against the South, he joined Quantrill's Raiders.

William Quantrill's forces did not belong to the regular army. Fighting as guerrillas, they broke most of the rules of war. They often attacked peaceful towns without warning. Their sudden strikes left burning houses and dead Union soldiers in their wake.

Hit-and-run raids stung the Union army, but did not defeat it. In 1862, army troops drove the last rebel units from Missouri. The victory did not end the fighting, however. Both sides hungered for revenge. Riders from Kansas raided Missouri towns that favored the South. With the rebel army gone, it was up to Quantrill and his men to defend the state.

When Frank James first joined Quantrill, the Raiders had less than 250 men. Most were tough young horsemen who relished the guerrilla life. They burned bridges and attacked Union patrols. The cost of failure was high. Captured Raiders were lined up and shot by firing squads.

The war soon came to the Samuel place. Some Kansas troops rode up and asked Dr. Samuel to help them find Quantrill. The older man refused. Angered by his silence, the soldiers hung him from a tree. Dr. Samuel nearly died before they let him breathe again. Still he would not talk. The soldiers yanked him up again and again, with the same results. When they rode away, they left the luckless man hanging from the tree. Zerelda cut him down just in time.

As they left, the Kansans found Jesse plowing a remote field. They asked him the same questions, but he refused to talk. Hoping to break him down, the men

When he was just fourteen, Jesse (right) wanted to join Quantrill's Raiders. His brother Frank (left) already was a member. The Raiders told Jesse to wait until he was sixteen.

whipped him with a rope. The blows slashed Jesse's back and left his shirt stained red with blood.

After the soldiers left, Jesse vowed to take revenge. He tried to join up with Quantrill, but the Raiders turned him down. He was too young, they said. Then word got out that Jesse had been to see Quantrill. Zerelda and Susan were thrown in jail for a few weeks.

The Raiders let Jesse join when he turned sixteen. He was assigned to a unit led by Bloody Bill Anderson. Jesse was a slim, dark-haired young man who still looked like a boy. A childhood illness made his pale-blue eyes blink more often than usual. Despite his youthful looks, Jesse proved to be a natural soldier. When he went into battle, he fought like a tiger.

Jesse earned a nickname when a pistol fired while he was cleaning it. The bullet sliced off the tip of his left middle finger. A startled Jesse yelled, "That's the dod-dingus pistol I ever saw!" From then on, his friends liked to call him Dingus. To cover the missing fingertip, Jesse took to wearing a glove.

In August 1864, Jesse was shot in the lung. The wound was painful, but it healed in a few weeks. Jesse rejoined Anderson in time to take part in a raid on Centralia, Missouri. The Raiders looted the town and shot captured Union soldiers. Fresh Union troops tracked the Raiders and attacked their camp. As the battle raged, Jesse shot the Union commander. It was his first kill—but it would not be his last.

CHAPTER THREE

JESSE BEGINS LIFE AS AN OUTLAW

Centralia was Bloody Bill Anderson's last big battle. After that, the Raiders broke up under Union pressure. Jesse joined a band that moved south to Texas. The men spent the winter of 1864 there.

The Civil War was coming to a close. The South's Robert E. Lee told his men to lay down their arms in April 1865. One by one, the other rebel armies gave up. Frank James and the last few Raiders followed Quantrill into Kentucky. They hoped to escape the firing squad by giving up there. Quantrill was killed before he could surrender. Frank and the others turned themselves in.

The news that the war had ended was slow to reach Texas. When it came, the band of Raiders hiding there knew their time had come. Would the Union troops treat them fairly?

Jesse and the others headed north to Missouri. As they neared Lexington, Jesse rode ahead. He carried

After Jesse was shot by Union troops in 1865, he was sent to Kansas City, Missouri, to recover at his uncle's home. Kansas City is pictured here in the 1850s.

a white flag to show that he was unarmed. Even so, the first Union troops he met opened fire. A bullet knocked Jesse off his horse. He tried to escape by crawling into the woods. Union soldiers chased him, eager for the kill. They turned back when Jesse shot one of their horses.

Jesse was soon burning with fever. Hoping to find relief, he spent the night in a cool creek. He woke up weak and in pain. A farm worker found him and took him into town. After a doctor treated his chest wound, a Union major paid a visit. The major could have arrested him. Instead, he paid a wagon driver to take Jesse to Kansas City, where the young man's uncle lived.

Jesse was near death when he reached his mother in Nebraska a month later. Zerelda had moved there after she and the younger children left Kearney. She nursed her son for eight long weeks. Despite her loving care, the wound was slow to heal.

Still wracked with pain, Jesse yearned for home. He said he did not want to die in a Northern state. Zerelda helped him board a steamboat. In Kansas City, Jesse was

Jesse's mother, Zerelda, tried to nurse her injured son back to health in Nebraska.

cared for by a pretty cousin. Zee Mimms and Jesse fell in love. They planned to wed as soon as his wound healed.

Thanks to Zee, Jesse was soon well enough to travel. A wagon carried him back to the Samuel place. Dr. Samuel, Zerelda, and Frank were already there, working the farm. Safe on his home soil, Jesse grew strong again. One by one, a gang of friends from the war days joined him. None of them were looking for honest work.

As his health improved, Jesse made plans for his future. The hard life of a farmer held little appeal. He decided to live by his guns, as he had during the war. Robbing banks and trains might lead to jail or an early grave. On the plus side, the outlaw life offered excitement and easy money.

The young outlaw said he would go where the money was. In his mind, that meant robbing banks. In the 1860s this was a bold new scheme. Banks, people believed, were as safe as churches. Outlaws had to be content with less risky targets.

All that changed on February 13, 1866. Jesse picked Liberty, Missouri, for his first robbery. He knew the town well. It was only a dozen miles from the Samuel place.

Ten men rode into Liberty on that cold winter morning. They halted their horses in front of the Clay County Savings Bank. Two of the men jumped down

Jesse chose the Clay County Savings Bank in Liberty, Missouri, for his first bank robbery. This photo of the bank was taken a century later in the 1980s.

and walked into the bank. A third man held the horses. His friends kept watch.

The bank had just opened. Cashier Greenup Bird and his son William looked up when the men walked in. One bearded man warmed his hands at the stove. The second man asked for change for a ten-dollar bill. Before Greenup could move, the man drew a gun.

After Jesse hit his first bank in Liberty, Missouri, a posse like this one set out in pursuit of the gang. That was common practice in the Wild West, where lawmen were few and far between. This is a posse that saddled up to pursue a later band of bank robbers.

"I'd like all the money in the bank," he said. Greenup never said so, but he may have known the man was Jesse James.

The second gunman aimed a pistol at William. "Make a noise and we will shoot you down," he warned.

The outlaws led Greenup and William back to the vault. The outlaws knew the money was kept in that iron strongroom. They forced William to scoop gold and silver coins into a wheat sack. The second man emptied a tin box that stood on the cashier's desk. The sack soon bulged with more than $60,000 in cash and bonds.

The outlaws pushed the Birds into the vault and slammed the door. "Stay in there! Don't you know all Birds should be caged?" the leader yelled. Laughing at their own joke, the gunmen ran out to their horses.

The outlaws filled the air with gunfire as they rode out of town. The wild barrage sent people ducking for safety. A college student named George Wymore did not duck fast enough. One of the gang members killed him with four quick shots.

The bank robbers headed south, stopping only to split the money. They threw away the bonds, which could not be turned into cash. Riding fast, they crossed the Missouri River by ferry and then broke up. Back in Liberty, men formed a posse to follow the gang. The chase ended when they lost the trail in the snow.

The posse did not stop at the Samuel place. The few people who had seen Jesse and Frank that morning kept quiet. They knew the James boys would shoot anyone who talked to the sheriff.

CHAPTER FOUR

JESSE JAMES, TRAIN ROBBER

After that first job, Jesse James went on a bank-robbing spree. The gang hit seven banks in three states. They even held up the box office at the Kansas City Fair.

As the years passed, Jesse and Frank added trains to their target list. That was a popular move in those days. Many people hated the railroads. High freight charges made it hard for farmers and ranchers to make a profit. They begged lawmakers to pass laws that would lower the rates. Railroad owners, in turn, bought enough votes to keep rate-fixing laws off the books.

The Reno brothers pulled off the first train robbery in 1866. Seven years later, Jesse and Frank hit a train of their own. They had learned how to reduce the risks during the war. Jesse picked the Chicago, Rock Island & Pacific Railroad for their first job. Frank had heard that one of its trains carried a safe full of gold. Jesse laid plans to stop that train near Adair, Iowa.

Brothers Jesse (right) and Frank (left) forged a successful bank and train robbery partnership. They are pictured here with their mother, Zerelda.

Jesse told his gang to pull up one of the rails. He knew the train would stop if the track was torn up. The engineer saw the danger, but put on the brakes too late. The engine tipped over, crushing him. Two masked robbers ran up and forced the mail car clerk to open the safe. They found only $2,000 inside. The gold was on a train due to pass the next day.

The gang also robbed the train's passengers. They took watches, money, and jewels. Some stories claim that Jesse never stole from pretty women. That is pure fiction. Jesse did like pretty women, but he stole from anyone who possessed something of value.

In 1874, the gang stopped a train at Gads Hill, Missouri. The outlaws robbed the passengers, cut open

Train robberies were still a new idea when the James brothers stopped their first train in 1873. The robbery pictured here took place in 1870.

the mail sacks, and cleaned out the safe. This time, the gang rode away with more than $10,000.

Before he left, Jesse handed a note to a trainman. It was a story for the newspapers. The headline read: "THE MOST DARING ROBBERY ON RECORD." Jesse had written the story to make sure the papers got the facts straight. He liked to read about his crimes.

After a holdup, the train crew often asked local farmers to form a posse. The reply would come back,

"Go chase 'em yourself. It ain't my money they stole."
Nevertheless, a few posses were formed. They gave up
when the trail led to Clay County. The locals knew better
than to help lawmen chase down Jesse and Frank James.

By now, Jesse and his gang had friends all over
Missouri. Many people were still angry over losing the
Civil War. Outlaws who robbed Northern banks and
trains were seen as heroes. Jesse's growing fame also
drew new recruits. The best known were the three
Younger brothers.

The James brothers' gang included brothers Cole, Bob, and Jim
Younger. Left to right: Cole Younger, Jesse James, Bob Younger,
and Frank James.

The Pinkerton Detective Agency was turned loose on the James gang in 1871. Agents stayed on the gang's trail for several years. Three "Pinkertons," as they were called, are pictured here.

The gang also needed friends. It helped to know farmers who would give them a meal and a place to sleep. Before they left, the outlaws paid for their room and board with gold. The farmers smiled when they saw the coins. They could work all year and not earn that much money.

Before they rode away, the leader would shake the farmer's hand. "You know, I'm Jesse James," he liked to say.

The banks and railroads wanted to hang Jesse, not shake his hand. When lawmen failed to catch him, the owners turned elsewhere. In 1871, a bank hired the Pinkerton Detective Agency. Robert Pinkerton followed the gang's trail almost to Kearney, then turned back. He said too many locals were willing to lie for the James boys.

The Pinkertons did not give up. In 1874, a young agent showed up in Liberty. John Whicher bragged that he was there to arrest Jesse and Frank. Despite his soft hands and city ways, Whicher claimed to be a farmer. He hoped to get a job at the Samuel place so he could spy on Jesse. A few days later, Whicher's body was found near Kearney. He had been shot through the heart.

That spring, Jesse and Zee Mimms agreed that it was time to marry. The cousins had been in love for nine years. The families tried to stop them, but Jesse and Zee had their minds made up. They were married in April by Jesse's uncle.

The new husband had a price on his head. One bank had put up $3,000 for his capture. The railroads added $5,000. This was big money. In those days, men worked twelve-hour days for only a dollar.

After a nine-year courtship, Zee Mimms and Jesse James were married in 1874.

Lured by the reward money, the Pinkertons returned. In early 1875, nine agents sneaked up on the Samuel place. They found two sweaty horses in the barn. The sight of the horses convinced them that Frank and Jesse must be in the house. One agent lit the fuse of a kerosene bomb and tossed it into the kitchen. Dr. Samuel saw the bomb and tried to kick it into the fireplace. He was too late. The blast killed Archie, Jesse's eight-year-old half brother, and injured Zerelda. A few days later a doctor had to cut off her arm.

Were Frank and Jesse home that day? No one knows for sure. They may have escaped by jumping from an upstairs window. What is sure is that someone opened fire as the Pinkertons ran off. One of the agents was wounded and died soon afterward.

The news of the bombing angered the public. Their rage was not directed at the James gang. Jesse never harmed women or killed children, did he?

Despite the close call, the robberies went on. Jesse and Frank hit banks, trains, and stagecoaches. Governor Thomas Crittenden vowed to rid Missouri of the outlaws. He put up another $5,000 for the capture of the James boys. Jesse's luck, however, turned bad long before someone could collect the reward.

CHAPTER FIVE

DISASTER AT NORTHFIELD

By 1876, Jesse and Frank James had pulled off a long string of holdups. Even so, many people still believed in them. The James boys, their friends argued, were honest men. Their only crime, it was said, was having ridden with Quantrill. Newspapers helped by printing Jesse's letters. In them, he always claimed that he had been somewhere else when the robberies took place.

More facts, however, were coming out. Lawmen

Jesse often wrote letters to newspapers explaining how he was innocent of the many robberies charged to him. Many people believed Jesse.

The James gang tried to rob a bank in Northfield, Minnesota, in 1876. The bungled holdup ended in disaster for the gang. This photo of Northfield was taken around the time of the robbery.

captured gang member Hobbs Kerry after a train robbery. Hobbs talked freely to his captors. He named Jesse, Frank, and the Younger brothers as gang members.

The gang's luck ran out in the fall of 1876. That was when Jesse led seven gang members north to check out targets in Minnesota. A bank in Northfield soon caught his eye.

Jesse, Bob Younger, and Sam Wells reached the bank first. Cole Younger rode up next and stopped in the middle of the street. He seemed to be fixing his saddle. Clell Miller joined Jesse, and the four outlaws walked into the bank. Frank, Jim Younger, and Bill Chadwell stayed back as a rear guard.

The trouble started when Clell let a man slip out of the bank. The man ran off, shouting that the bank was being robbed. A store owner grabbed his rifle and opened fire. Frank and his two friends galloped toward the bank, pistols drawn. Bullets whizzed past their heads. A dozen or so Northfield men had opened fire.

Inside the bank, the robbery had hit another snag. Bank clerk Joseph Heywood tried to slam the vault door on Sam Wells. Sam barely escaped being locked inside. Jesse then ordered Heywood to open the safe. The quick-thinking clerk pointed to a time lock. The safe cannot be opened, he said. In truth, the safe was unlocked, but Jesse did not have time to check. A second clerk was running toward the back door. Wells shot him in the arm, but the man kept on running.

Jesse heard the gunfire in the street. It was time to go. On the way out, he shot the helpless Heywood.

Chadwell and Miller lay dead in the street. Frank had a leg wound. Cole and Jim Younger had both been hit. Cole pulled Bob Younger up behind him, and the gang galloped away. Behind them, church bells rang the alarm.

Day after day, a posse chased the gang. When their horses wore out, the outlaws stole fresh mounts. After several days, they split up. Jesse and Frank escaped into Iowa. A week later, the posse caught up with the others. Sam Wells died in a fierce gun battle. The three Youngers were captured and thrown in jail.

The failure at Northfield troubled Jesse. For the first time, townsfolk had turned on him. It seemed best to lie low and wait for better times.

Jesse and Frank slowly worked their way back home. Frank went to Fulton to have his wound treated. That same night, Frank's doctor and Jesse ate in the town's hotel. One story says they shared a table with some Pinkerton men. The Pinkertons were looking for the James brothers, but no one gave Jesse away. Cool as always, Jesse very likely enjoyed the close call.

Jesse and Frank moved on to a hideout in Texas. They called it their Rest Ranch. Frank settled in with his books, but Jesse was restless. It seems likely

Gang member Jim Younger was shot in the disastrous bank robbery in Northfield, Minnesota, in 1876.

that he led Frank on trips into Mexico. On one visit they ran into soldiers who hoped to collect the reward money. Jesse and Frank shot their way out of the trap.

Jesse's wife and their two children, Jesse Edwards (rear) and Mary (front), stayed in Tennessee while Jesse continued his crime spree in the late 1870s and early 1880s.

Jesse was not fond of shoot-outs. He knew he was not a marksman. He once fired six times at a man and missed each time. When he did kill someone it was likely to be at close range.

By now, Jesse and Zee had a son, Jesse Edwards James. When the brothers came back from Texas, they packed their families into wagons. The journey led them east to Tennessee, a trip of five hundred miles. In August 1877, Jesse found a home in Waverly. Frank lived a long day's ride away in Nashville.

Jesse used the name J. D. Howard. He joined the church and sang in the choir. When the county fair races began, he entered his horse, Red Fox. Red Fox won a number of races for his proud owner. Zee gave birth to twins, but the babies died soon after birth.

Jesse made his home on a farm, but he still disliked hard work. He lived on the cash from his holdups. After two years the money ran low. Jesse moved Zee and the baby to a house in Nashville. His neighbors thought he was in the wheat business. When little Jesse was four, Zee gave birth to a baby girl. They named her Mary.

Frank worked for a lumber company. He saved his money and rented a farm where he raised hogs and horses. Jesse and his family joined Frank on the farm. Jesse, restless as always, took off to visit a friend in New Mexico.

When Jesse came back, Frank said he was tired of the outlaw life. He tried to convince Jesse they could make their living by working the farm. Jesse turned him down. He was ready to return to his real "work"— robbing banks and trains.

CHAPTER SIX

THE END OF THE TRAIL

Jesse's first task was to round up a new gang. The old crew was out of action. The Younger brothers were in prison. Sam Wells and Bill Chadwell were dead. Clell Miller's bones were hanging in a Northfield doctor's office.

The word went out that Jesse needed men. Ed Miller, Clell's brother, joined up. Then Wood Hite, Jesse's cousin, signed on. Tucker Bassham, Bill Ryan, and Dick Liddil also joined.

By 1879 Jesse had tired of trying to make an honest living. He put out the word and quickly rounded up a new gang.

The new James gang pulled its first job in the fall of 1879. Glendale, Missouri, was the target. When they arrived, the outlaws found most of the townsfolk in Glendale's one store. With guns drawn, the outlaws herded their captives into the train station. Jesse smashed the telegraph while the others laid logs on the track. When the incoming train braked to a stop, the gang took $6,000 from the mail car. Before he left, Jesse told the men on the train who he was. Jesse James was back!

Jesse gave each gang member his share of the loot. Then he made the long ride back to Nashville. A few neighbors must have wondered where he had been. None of them knew that the quiet Mr. Howard was really Jesse James.

The new gang soon split up. Tucker Bassham bragged too loudly that he was part of the James gang. When captured, he confessed that he had taken part in the Glendale holdup. Later, Bill Ryan was put on trial for the same crime. Bassham won his freedom by naming Ryan as part of the gang.

Jesse shrugged off the setback. In the fall of 1880, he and a friend robbed a stagecoach in Kentucky. The two men rode off with a gold watch, a diamond ring, and a wad of cash.

PROCLAMATION
$5,000⁰⁰

REWARD

FOR EACH of SEVEN ROBBERS of THE TRAIN at WINSTON, MO., JULY 15, 1881, and THE MURDER of CONDUCTER WESTFALL

$ 5,000.00
ADDITIONAL for ARREST or CAPTURE

DEAD OR ALIVE
OF JESSE OR FRANK JAMES

THIS NOTICE TAKES the PLACE of ALL PREVIOUS REWARD NOTICES.

CONTACT SHERIFF, DAVIESS COUNTY, MISSOURI IMMEDIATELY

T. T. CRITTENDEN, GOVERNOR
STATE OF MISSOURI
JULY 26, 1881

In 1881, Frank James once again teamed up with Jesse. Soon posters all over Missouri were offering generous rewards for the capture of the two James boys and their new gang.

While this was going on, Frank had a change of heart. He rejoined Jesse in July 1881. Jesse was ready with a new plan and a new gang. Everyone bought tickets and boarded the train they planned to rob. After the train left the station, Jesse pulled his gun.

Everyone froze, but he fired anyway. The bullet killed the conductor. In the meantime, his men were forcing their way into the mail car. One of them shot a clerk who looked as though he was about to flee. Then they cleaned out the safe.

The gang escaped, but Jesse's luck had run out. The outlaws had killed two men, but rode off with only $800. Gang member Ed Miller dropped from sight a few weeks later. People guessed that Jesse probably shot him for talking too much.

The gang's last job nearly ended in a train wreck. Jesse stopped a train he thought was carrying a large sack of cash. Instead, he found that the safe was nearly empty. With the train stopped, a second train came chugging down the same track. An alert brakeman ran up the track and stopped the oncoming engine just in time. Jesse gave the man a tip. He also gave the engineer two silver dollars to drink to his health.

Frank did not like the way things were going. He left the gang in the spring of 1882 and went back to his farm. The brothers never saw each other again.

Jesse was thirty-four years old when Frank left. He moved Zee and the children to St. Joseph, Missouri. They lived in a white house on a hill. Jesse used the name Thomas Howard and grew a beard.

With his cash almost gone, Jesse planned to rob a bank in Platte City, Missouri. He said he could do the job with a three-man gang. Zee thought he wanted the money to buy a farm.

Charlie Ford, a new member of the gang, liked the plan. In late March, Jesse and Charlie met with Charlie's brother, Bob Ford. Bob said he would join them for the Platte City robbery. Later, he took Charlie aside. The smart thing, he said, would be to kill Jesse and claim the reward. Charlie agreed.

No one knows the whole story. Governor Crittenden and two policemen may have cut a deal with the Fords. Charlie and Bob, the rumors say, agreed to give them three-fourths of the $10,000 reward. In return, the officials promised to keep the Fords out of jail.

On April 3, the Fords joined Jesse and Zee for breakfast. Jesse gave Bob a new pistol and Charlie a new horse. Why did he trust the Fords? Most experts agree that Jesse must have guessed that the Fords might try to kill him. He had already caught Bob Ford lying to him. On top of that, there was that large reward. Jesse surely knew how tempting it was.

A younger Jesse would have driven the Fords out of his house. Now he was tired, and the law was hot on his trail. If he were caught he would be locked up. That thought was too much to bear. Jesse had always said, "They can kill me, but they will never send me to jail."

When the men moved to the living room, Jesse took off his gun belt. Then he turned his back on the Fords, saying that a picture needed dusting. As he climbed up on a chair, Bob and Charlie moved in behind him. Bob raised his

It is widely believed that Governor Thomas Crittenden of Missouri struck a deal with the Ford brothers to kill Jesse.

new pistol. The click of the gun being cocked made Jesse turn his head. Bob knew it was now or never. He pulled the trigger.

The bullet hit Jesse in the back of the head. He was dead when he crashed to the floor.

Zee rushed in from the kitchen. She screamed with rage and grief when she saw Jesse. The Fords ran out. Bob sent a telegram to the governor. It read: "I've got him, sure."

After Jesse's death on April 3, 1882, Bob Ford (above) was forever known as "that dirty little coward that shot Mr. Howard."

Bob and Charlie were tried and sentenced to death. Governor Crittenden, however, kept his word. He gave the killers a full pardon. What the Fords could not escape was the scorn of the public. From that day on, Bob Ford was known as "that dirty little coward that shot Mr. Howard."

CHAPTER SEVEN

THE ROBIN HOOD MYTH

Bob Ford killed Jesse James but he could not kill Jesse's myth. The stories grew as the years passed. Songs were written that turned the outlaw into a hero. One song told it this way:

> *Jesse James was one of his names,*
> *Another it was Howard.*
> *He robbed the rich of every stitch.*
> *You bet, he was no coward.*

Frank James outlived his brother by more than thirty years. He was put on trial for his crimes, but was set free by the jury. Frank helped build Jesse's myth by telling his own tall tales of their lives. He even charged tourists fifty cents to visit the Samuel place.

Why did the outlaw Jesse James become a hero? For one thing, Americans have always rooted for underdogs.

For another, the bitter feelings left by the Civil War helped build the myth. Many Southerners felt that Jesse was righting the wrongs done to them. Magazines called dime novels also added to his mystique. They ran story after story about Jesse. Most of them were fiction, but no one cared. Readers liked stories about outlaw heroes.

The myth further claims that Jesse stole only from the rich. That belief turned him into a homegrown Robin Hood. If this Robin Hood kept what he stole, no one seemed to care. People liked to see the rich and powerful taken down a peg. A second verse of the song added:

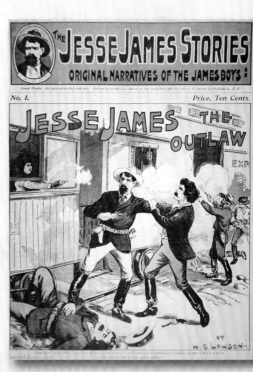

Jesse stole from the rich
And he gave to the poor.
He'd a hand and a heart
and a brain.

Was Jesse a villain or a hero? Was he a heartless killer or just a loving family man? Perhaps he was some of each. The whole truth may never be known.

Dime novels of the late 1800s helped build the legend of Jesse James by glorifying his "heroic" adventures.

GLOSSARY

bonds—Certificates that guarantee the holder a certain amount of money plus interest at a future date.

Civil War—The war fought between the North (the Union) and the South (the Confederacy), 1861–1865.

detective agency—A business that provides police services for anyone who pays its fees.

dime novels—Low-cost magazines that printed popular fiction during the late 1800s.

frontier—A region that is being opened to settlement. Life in a frontier area is often hard and dangerous.

guerrillas—Small, fast-moving military bands that operate outside the normal rules of warfare.

gunslingers—Outlaws and lawmen of the Wild West who settled arguments with their pistols.

kerosene—A liquid fuel often used for lamps.

militia—Lightly-trained citizens who are called to military duty to back up the regular army.

myth—A story that many people believe, but which is almost always untrue.

Pinkertons—Private detectives who worked for the famous Pinkerton Detective Agency.

posse—A group of citizens who join with law enforcement officers to aid in the capture of outlaws.

Quantrill's Raiders—A band of Southern guerrillas led by William Quantrill who fought against Union forces in Missouri.

telegraph—A communications device that was used before telephones became common. Telegraphers used Morse code to transmit electronic signals over networks of telegraph wires.

Union—The name given to the United States forces that fought against the South during the Civil War.

FURTHER READING

Books

Beights, Ronald H. *Jesse James and the First Missouri Train Robbery*. Gretna, La.: Pelican, 2002.

Frisch, Aaron. *Jesse James*. Mankato, Minn.: Creative Education, 2005.

Landau, Elaine. *Jesse James: Wild West Train Robber*. Berkeley Heights, N.J.: Enslow, 2004.

Robinson, J. Dennis. *Jesse James: Legendary Rebel and Outlaw*. Mankato, Minn.: Compass Point Books, 2006.

Internet Addresses

Spartacus Educational: Jesse James
http://www.spartacus.schoolnet.co.uk/WWjamesJ.htm

St. Joseph, Missouri, History—Jesse James
http://www.ci.st-joseph.mo.us/history/jessejames.cfm

INDEX